HAL•LEONARD®

GUITAR PLAY-ALONG

AUDIO ACCESS INCLUDED

SUBLIME

PLAYBACK+
Speed • Pitch • Balance • Loop

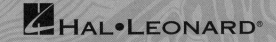

To access audio visit:
www.halleonard.com/mylibrary

Enter Code
4190-9165-9328-8776

Transcriptions by Joe Collinson

ISBN 978-1-70514-265-3

HAL•LEONARD®

Visit Hal Leonard Online at
www.halleonard.com

World headquarters, contact:
Hal Leonard
7777 West Bluemound Road
Milwaukee, WI 53213
Email: info@halleonard.com

In Europe, contact:
Hal Leonard Europe Limited
42 Wigmore Street
Marylebone, London, W1U 2RN
Email: info@halleonardeurope.com

In Australia, contact:
Hal Leonard Australia Pty. Ltd.
4 Lentara Court
Cheltenham, Victoria, 3192 Australia
Email: info@halleonard.com.au

Badfish

Words and Music by Brad Nowell

Intro
Moderately ♩ = 81

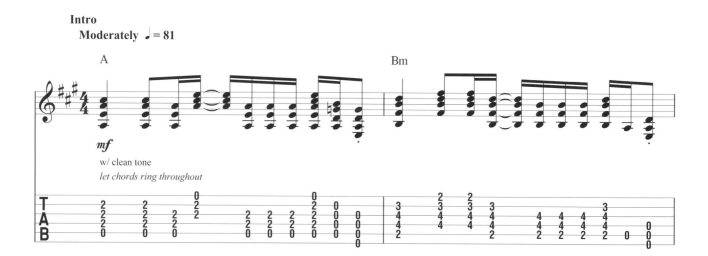

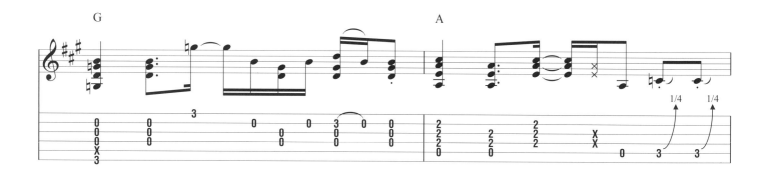

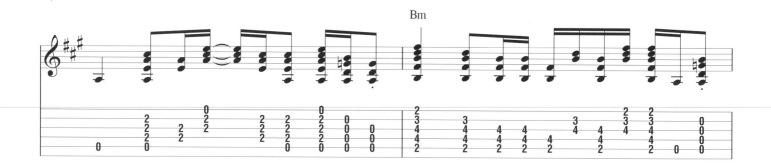

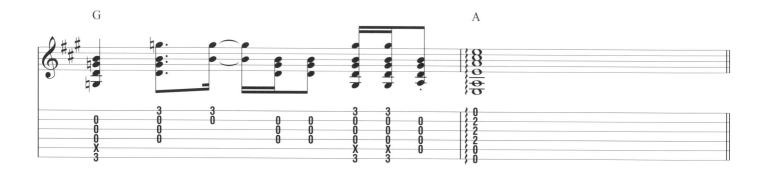

Lord _____ knows I'm _____ weak. _____ Won't some -

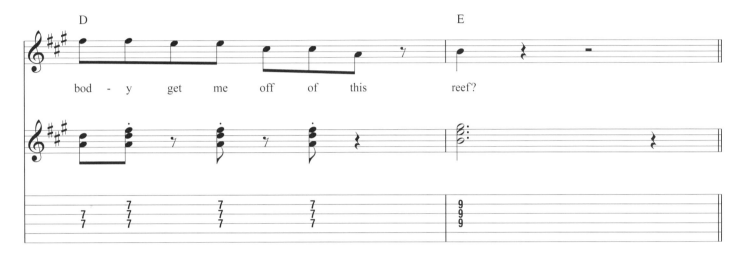

bod - y get me off of this reef?

Verse

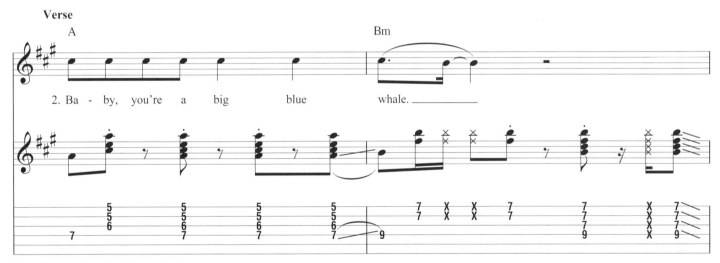

2. Ba - by, you're a big blue whale. _____

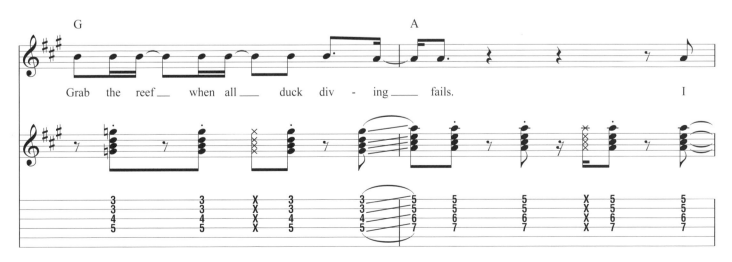

Grab the reef _____ when all _____ duck div - ing _____ fails.

I

swim, but I wish I'd nev - er learned. _____ The

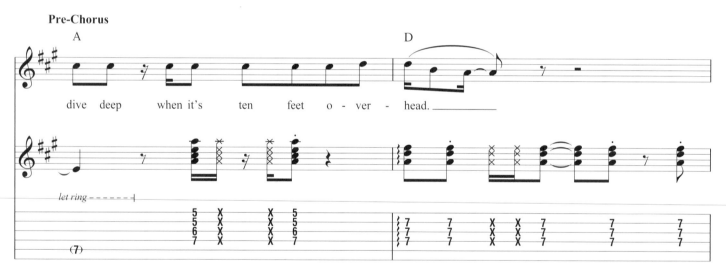

wa - ter's too pol - lu - ted with germs. I

Pre-Chorus

dive deep when it's ten feet o - ver - head. _____

Grab the reef _ un - der - neath _ my _____ bed. ...neath my bed but...
(It's un - der - neath my bed but...)

Chorus

Ain't got no quar - rels with God. ____

w/ reverse reverb

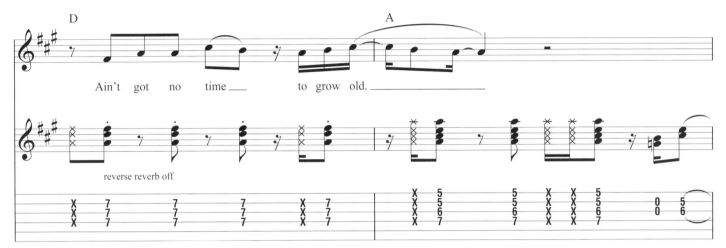

Ain't got no time ____ to grow old. ____

reverse reverb off

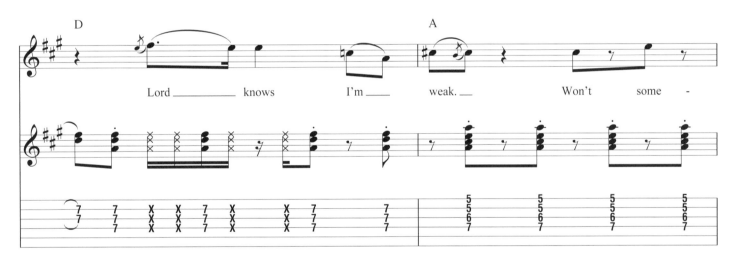

Lord ____ knows I'm ____ weak. ____ Won't some -

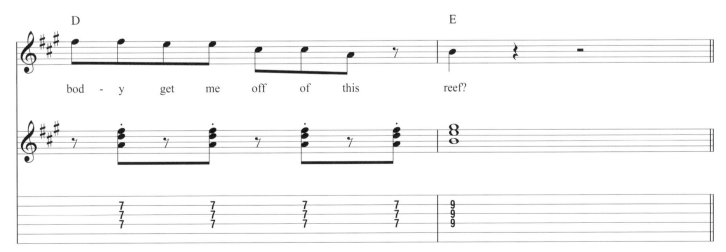

bod - y get me off of this reef?

Interlude

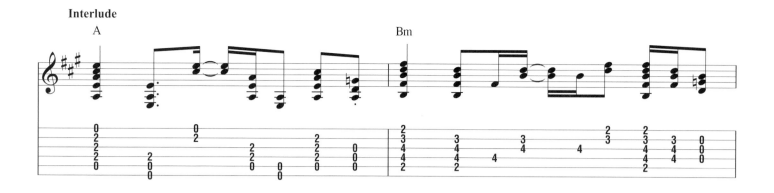

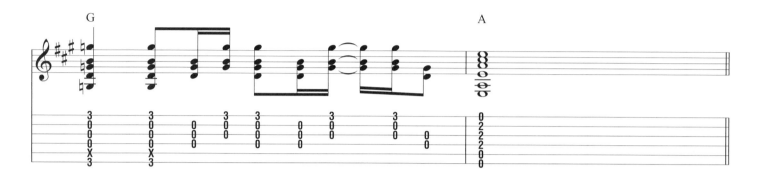

Guitar Solo

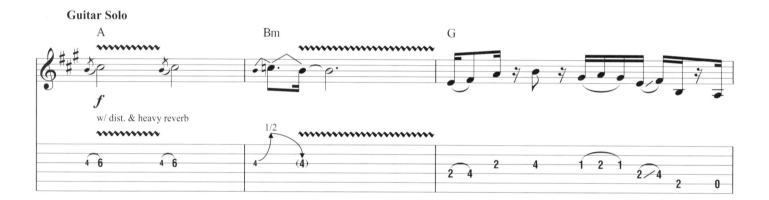

Chorus

Ain't got no quar-rels with God. ____

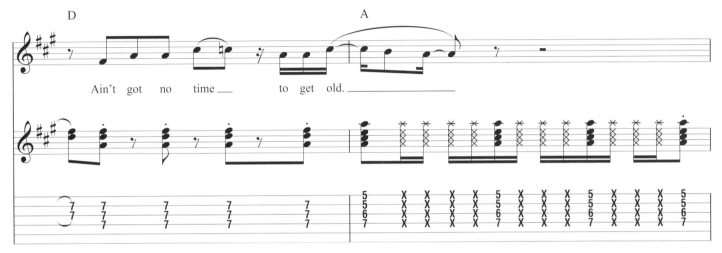

Ain't got no time ____ to get old. ____

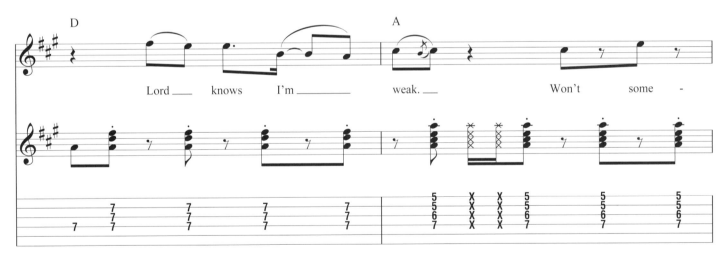

Lord ____ knows I'm _____ weak. ____ Won't some -

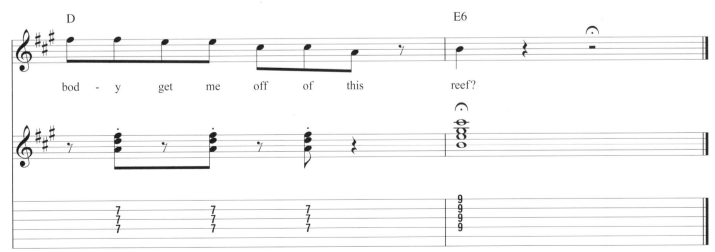

bod - y get me off of this reef?

Ebin

Words and Music by Brad Nowell

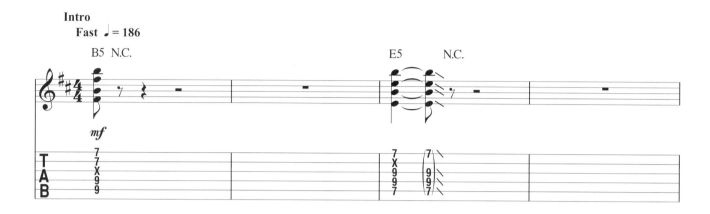

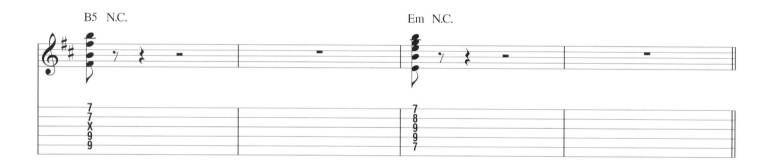

Verse
Faster ♩ = 193

1. Out my win-dow, cool and bright. _ Fade so slow-ly in - to night.

ten - nis shoes. _ Deal - in', he was look - in' for some - thin' to use. _ With a

pis - tol in his pock - et and a bot - tle of booze. _ Well, it could _ be me _ or it

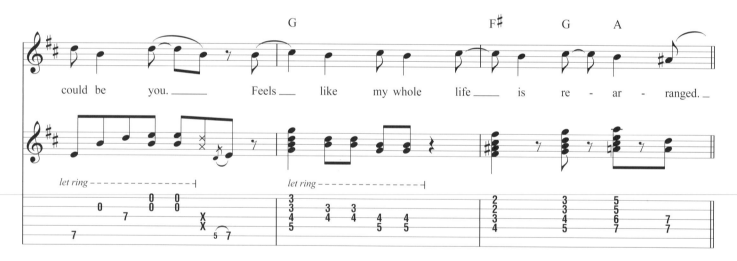

could be you. _ Feels _ like my whole life _ is re - ar - ranged. _

Chorus

Eb - in, you _

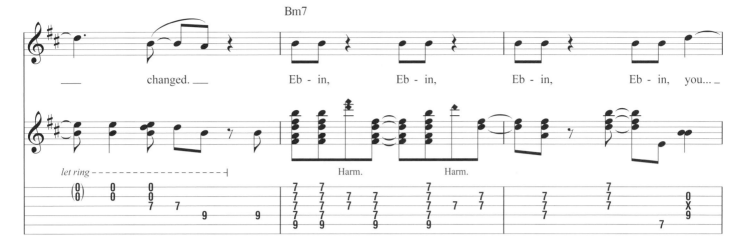

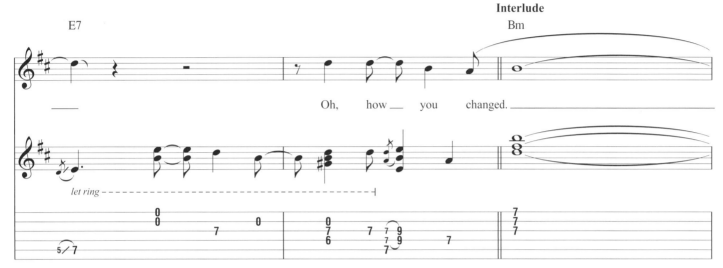

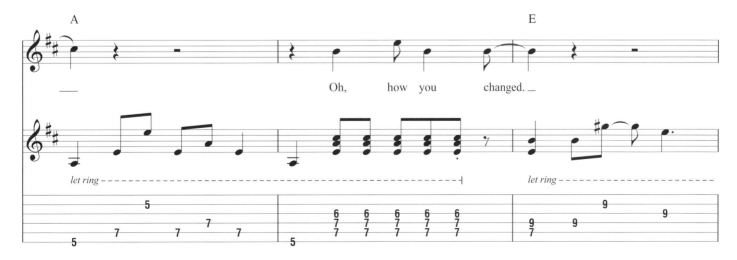

Bridge

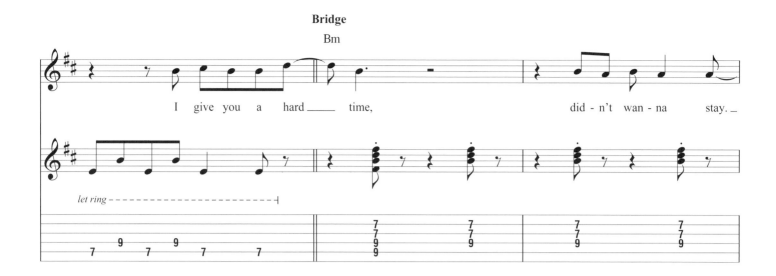

I give you a hard ____ time, did - n't wan - na stay. ___

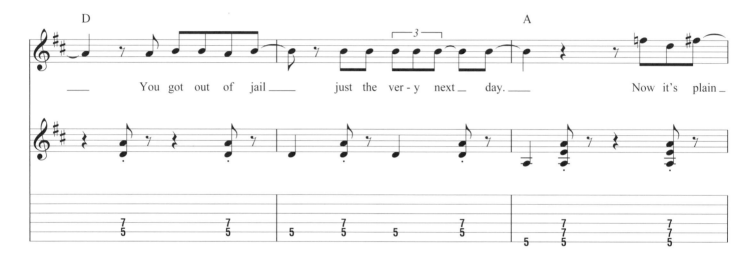

__ You got out of jail ___ just the ver - y next _ day. ___ Now it's plain _

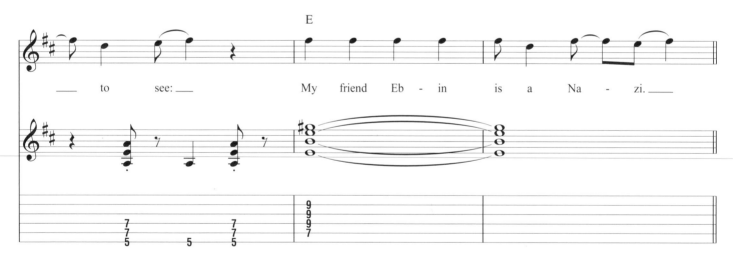

__ to see: ___ My friend Eb - in is a Na - zi. ___

Interlude

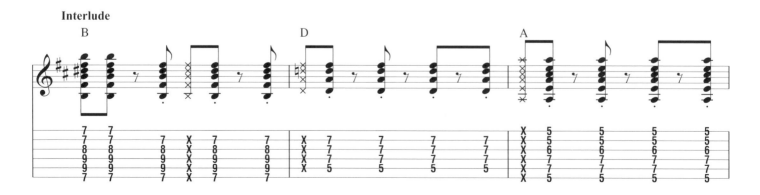

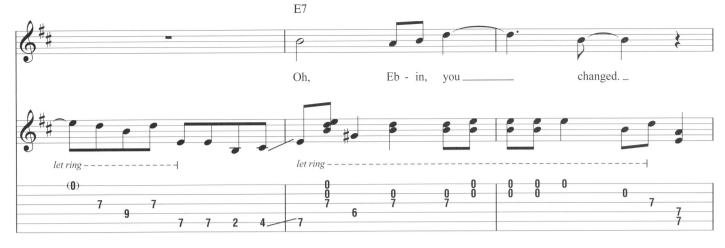

Oh, Eb - in, you ___ changed. _

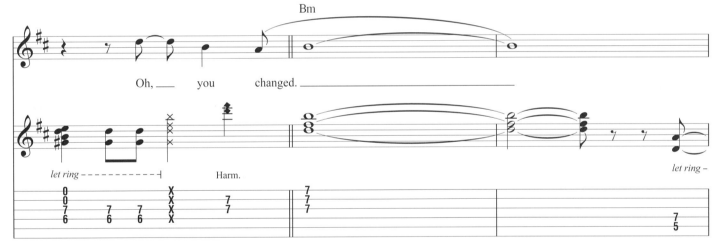

Eb - in, Eb - in, Eb - in, Eb - in, you... ___

Interlude

Oh, ___ you changed. _

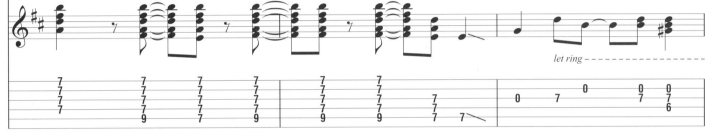

Oh, ___ you changed. _

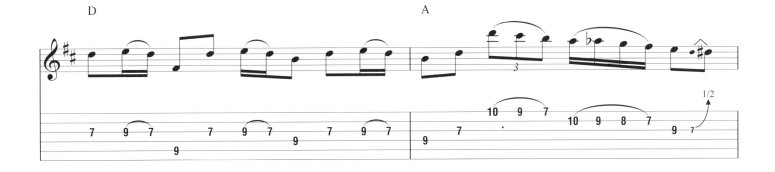

He was a Na - zi, yeah,__ yeah,__ yeah.__

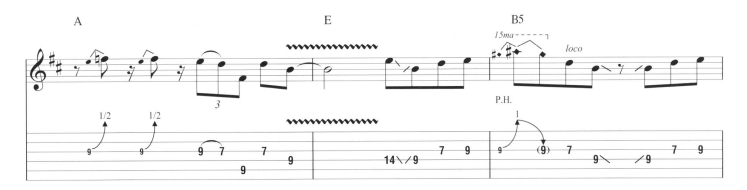

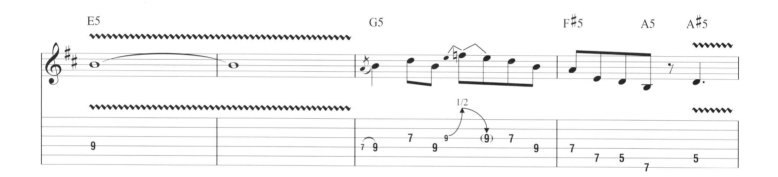

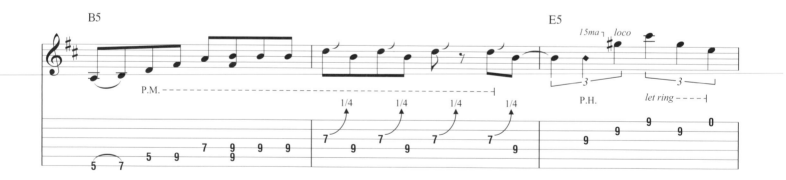

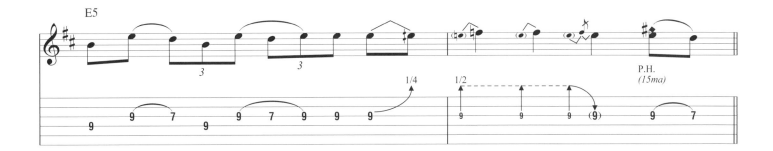

Verse

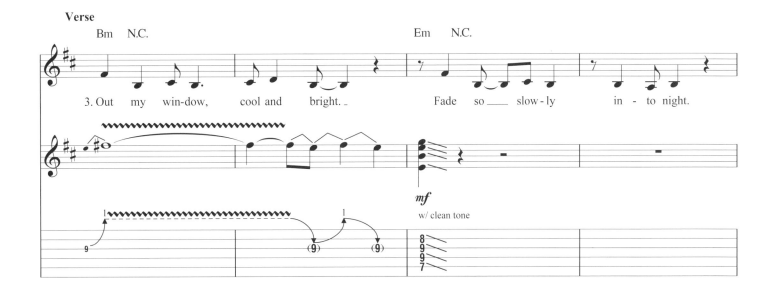

3. Out my win-dow, cool and bright. __ Fade so __ slow-ly in - to night.

mf
w/ clean tone

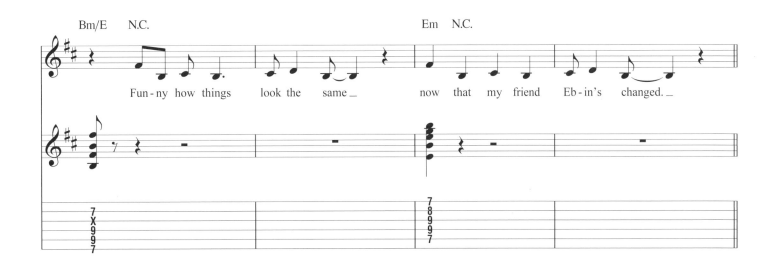

Fun-ny how things look the same __ now that my friend Eb-in's changed. __

Outro

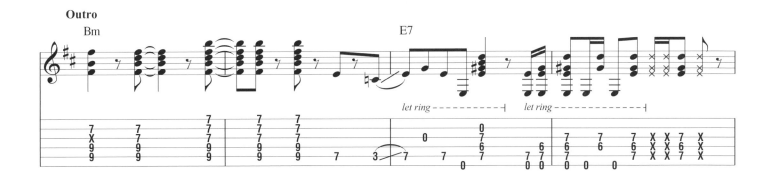

let ring --------- *let ring* ---------

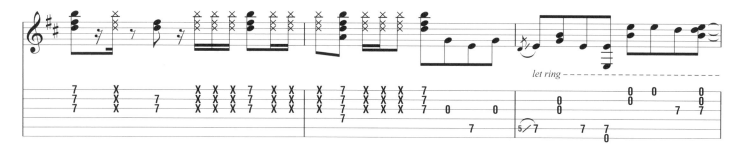

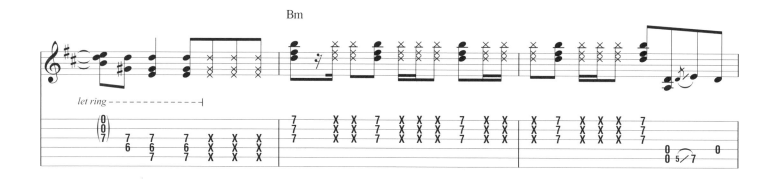

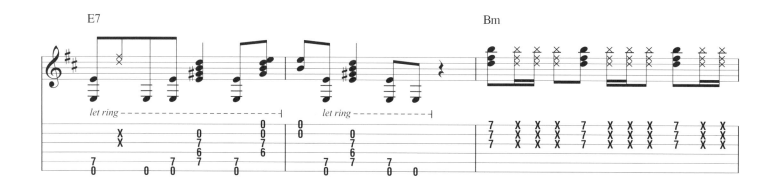

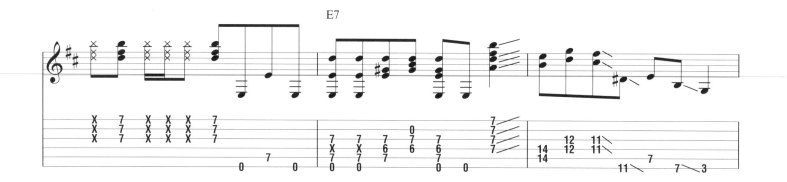

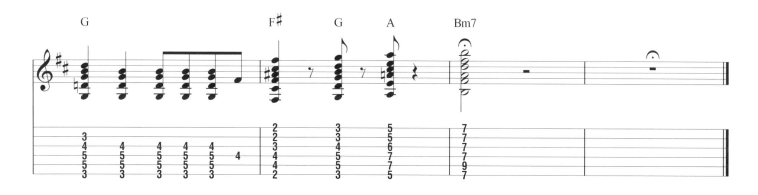

Pawn Shop

Words and Music by Brad Nowell, Eric Wilson, Floyd Gaugh, Winston Matthews and Lloyd MacDonald

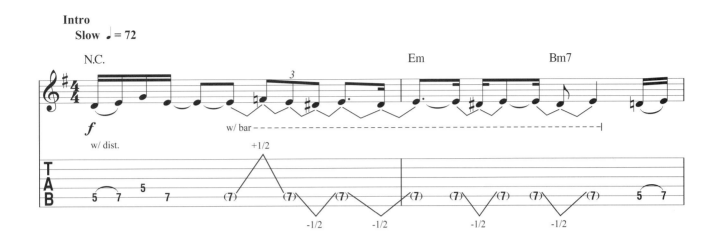

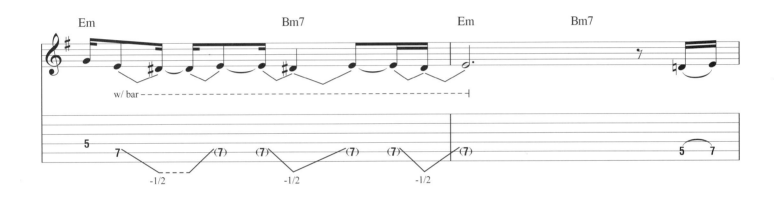

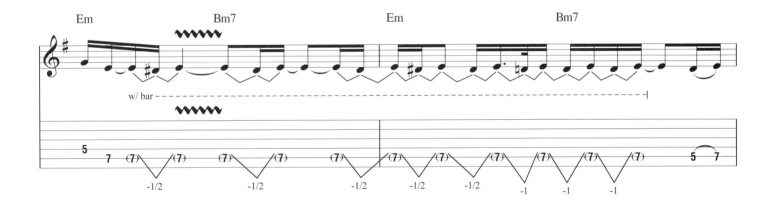

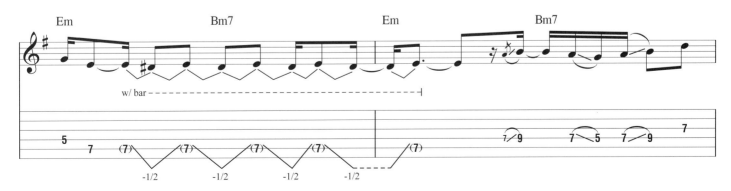

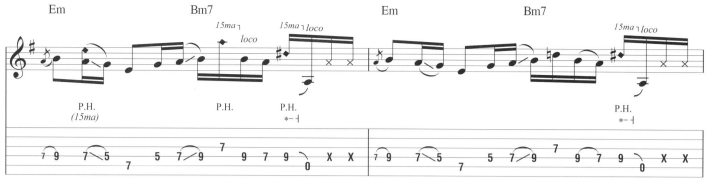

*w/ delay set for 16th-note regeneration with 6 repeats.

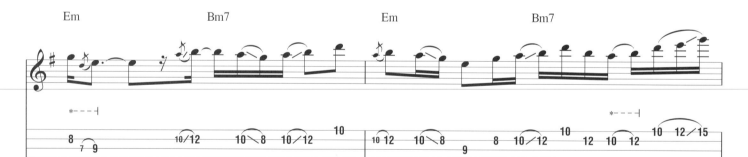

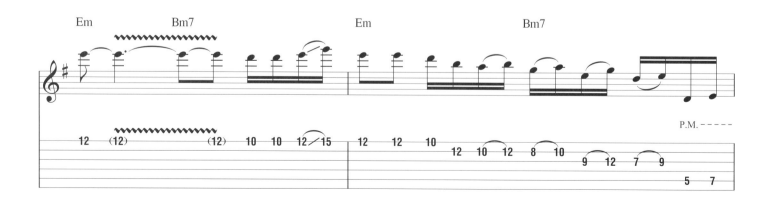

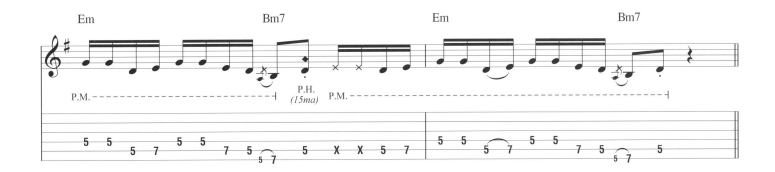

Chorus

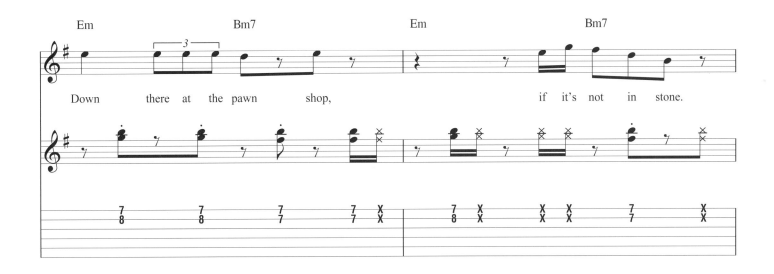

Down there at the pawn shop, ain't no way, no way to shop.

Down there at the pawn shop.

Verse

1. What has been _ told? Al - bi - no made of stone.

But just re-mem-ber that it's flesh and bone. __

Interlude

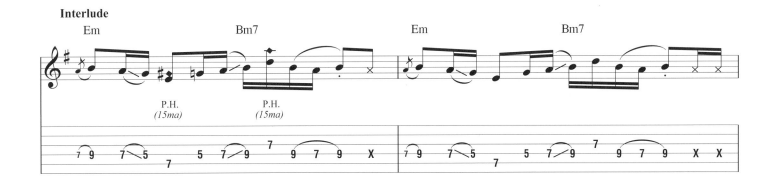

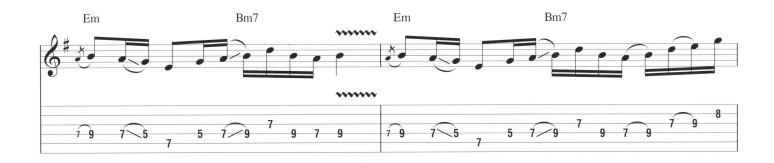

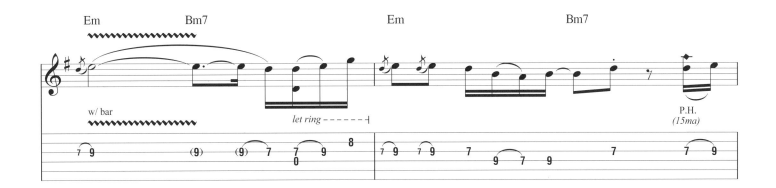

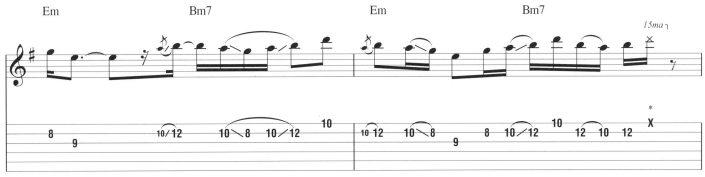

*Push pick into string above pickups.

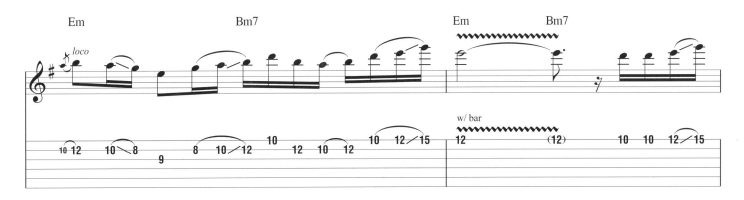

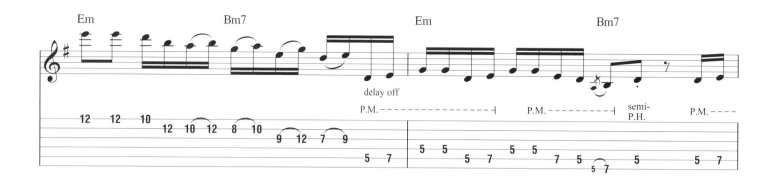

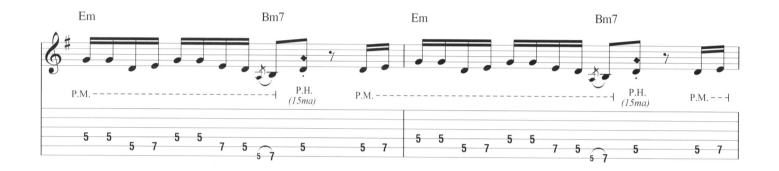

Chorus

So why I'm down here at the pawn shop.

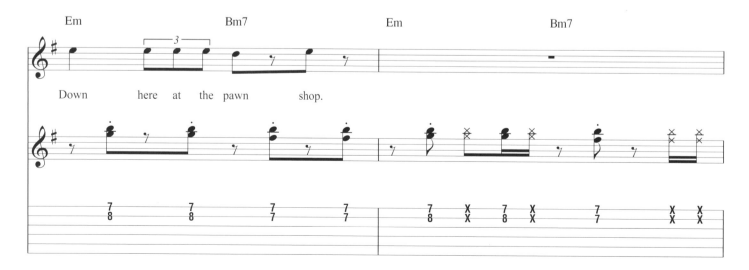

Down here at the pawn shop.

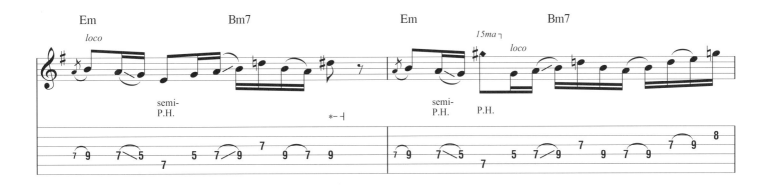

*w/ delay set for eighth-note triplet regeneration with 6 repeats.

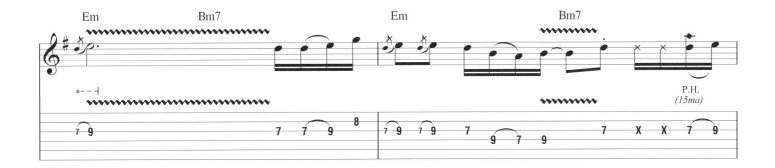

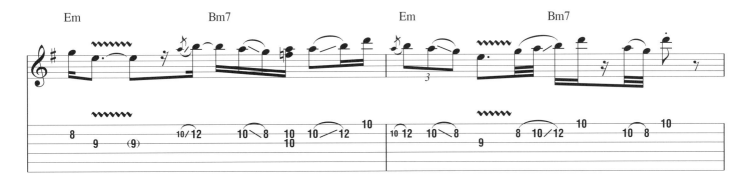

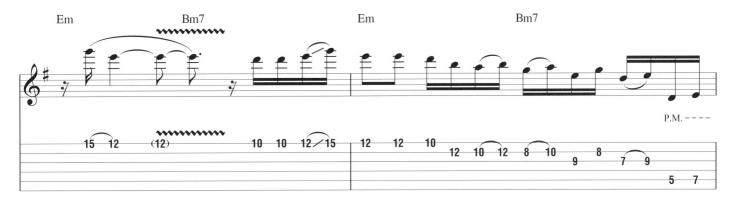

Chorus

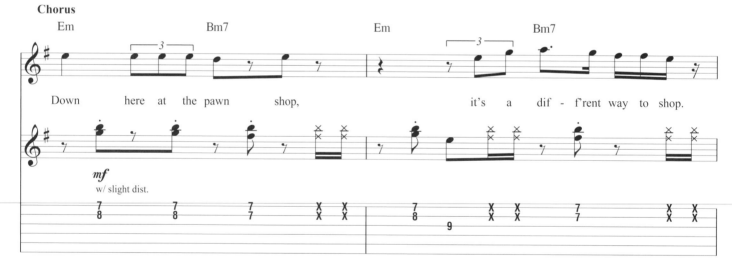

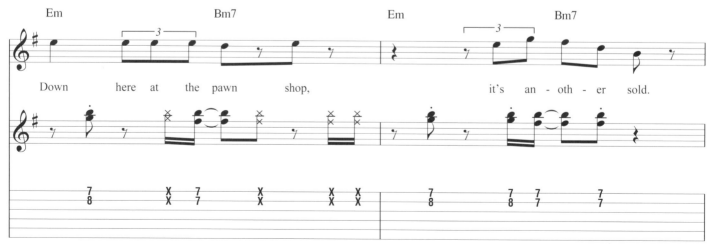

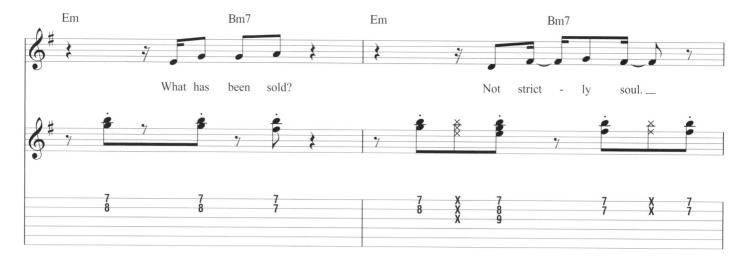

What has been sold? Not strict - ly soul. __

Please re - mem - ber it's flesh and bone. __ Why I'm

Outro-Chorus

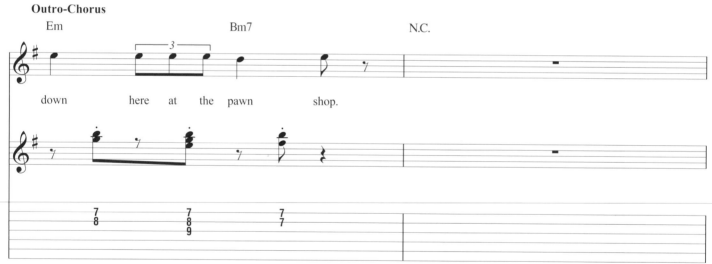

down here at the pawn shop.

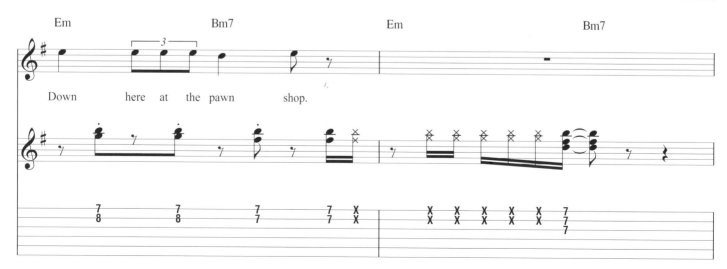

Down here at the pawn shop.

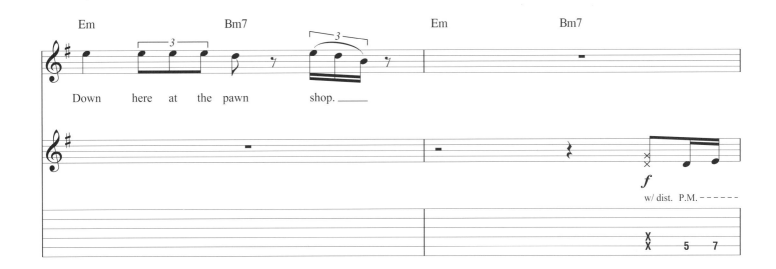

Down here at the pawn shop.____

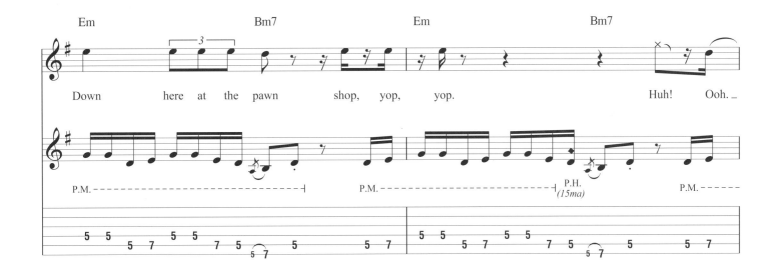

Down here at the pawn shop, yop, yop. Huh! Ooh.__

____ Go! Sing.

Santeria

Words and Music by Brad Nowell, Eric Wilson and Floyd Gaugh

San-cho that she's found, well, I'd pop a cap in San-cho and I'd slap her down.

Chorus

What I real-ly wan-na know, my ba-by, mm. What I real-ly wan-na say

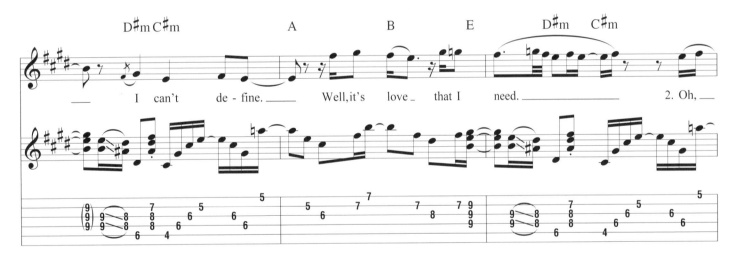

I can't de-fine. Well, it's love that I need. 2. Oh,

% Verse

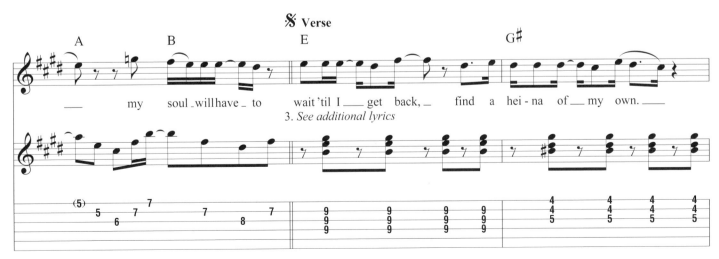

my soul will have to wait 'til I get back, find a hei-na of my own.
3. *See additional lyrics*

38

To Coda ⊕

Guitar Solo

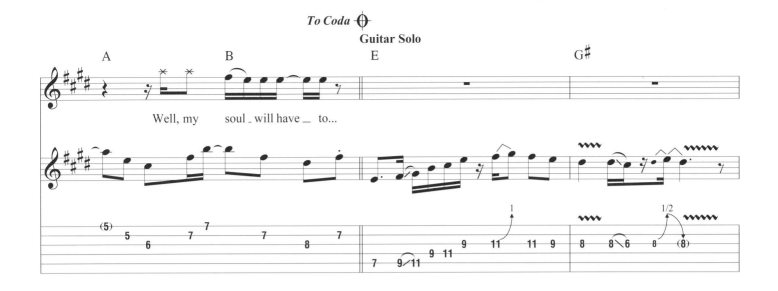

Well, my soul will have to...

Chorus

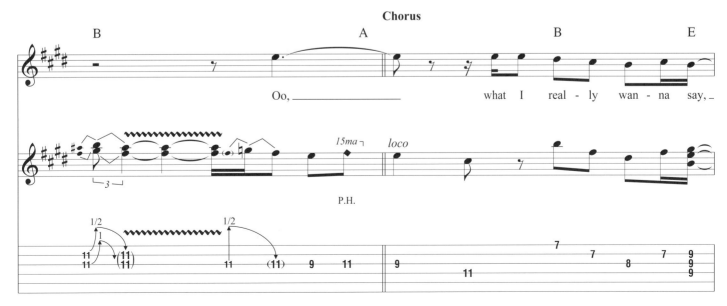

Oo, _____ what I real - ly wan - na say, _

39

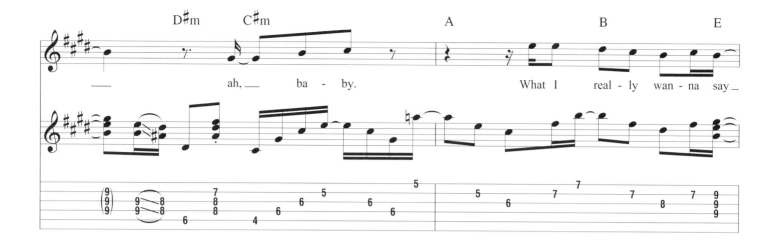

ah, ___ ba - by.   What I   real - ly wan - na say ___

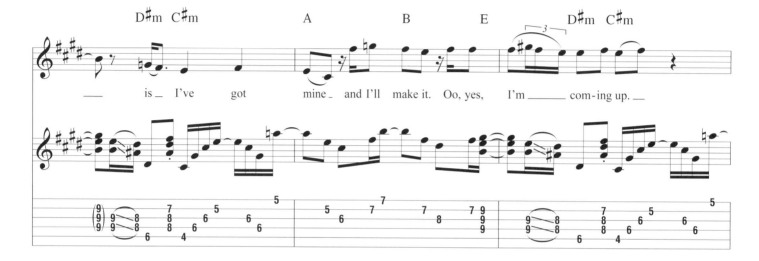

___ is ___ I've got mine ___ and I'll make it. Oo, yes, I'm _____ com - ing up. ___

D.S. al Coda

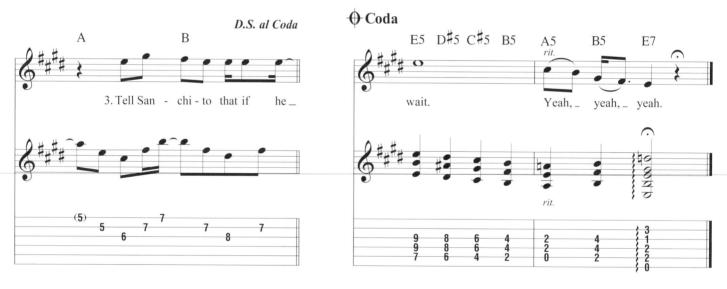

3. Tell San - chi - to that if he ___

⊕ **Coda**

wait.   Yeah, ___ yeah, ___ yeah.

Additional Lyrics

3. Tell Sanchito that if he knows what is good for him
   He best go run and hide.
   Daddy's got a new .45
   And I won't think twice to stick that barrel
   Straight down Sancho's throat.
   Believe me when I say that I
   Got something for his punk ass.

Chorus What I really wanna know, my baby.
   Oo, what I really wanna say is there's just
   One way back and I'll make it.
   Yeah, my soul will have to wait. Yeah, yeah, yeah.

Smoke Two Joints

Words and Music by Chris Kay and Michael Kay

Intro
Moderately slow ♩ = 95
Double-time feel

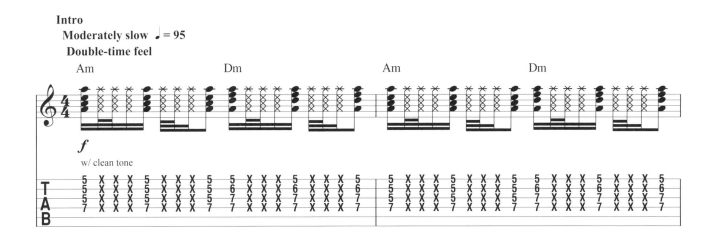

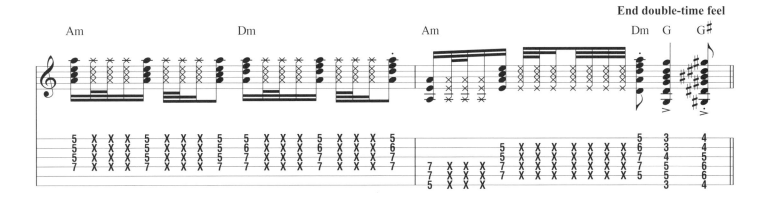

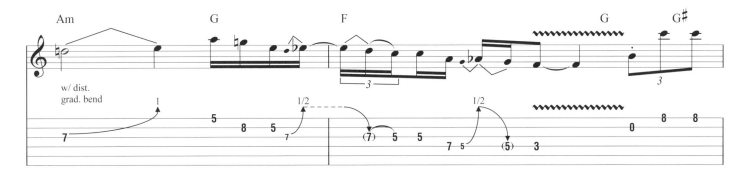

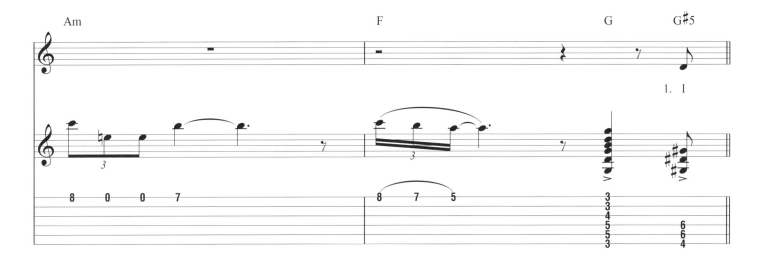

Interlude

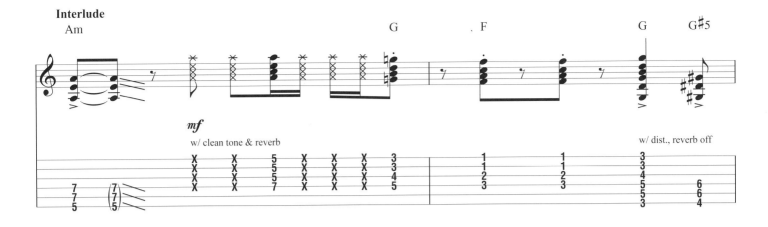

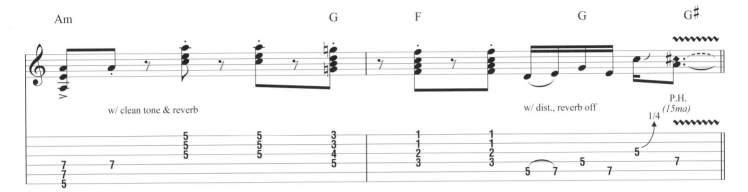

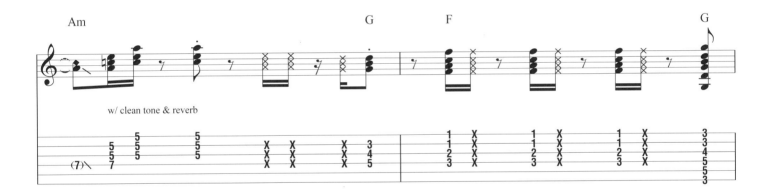

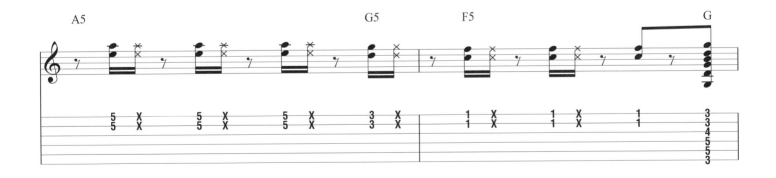

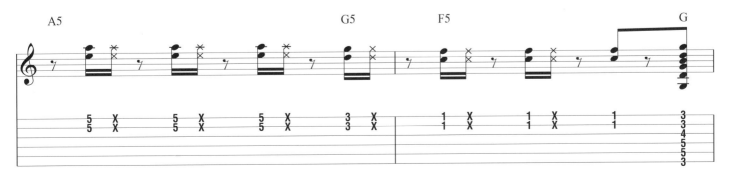

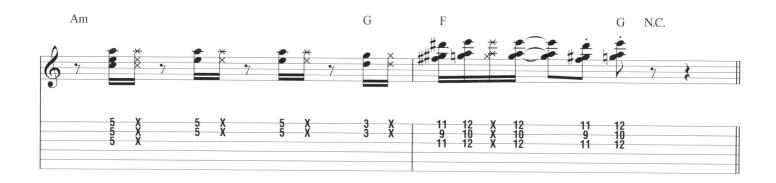

Verse

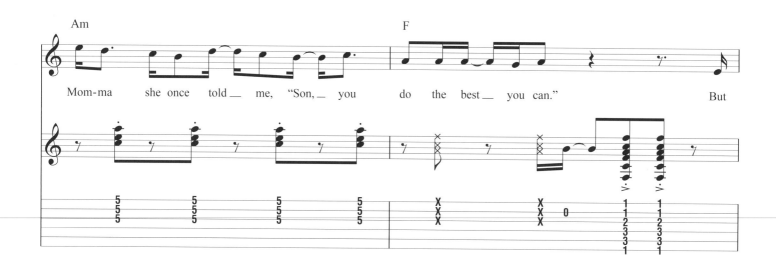

2. Dad - dy he once told __ me, "Son, __ you be hard work - in' man." __ And

Mom - ma she once told __ me, "Son, __ you do the best __ you can." But

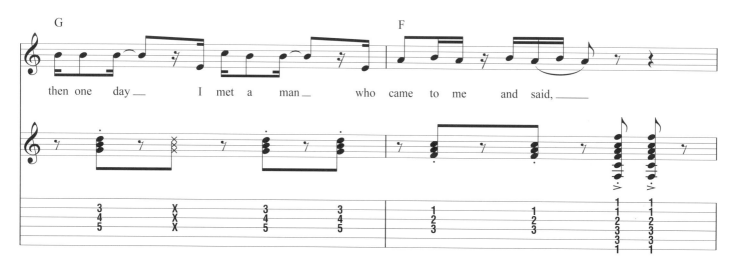

then one day __ I met a man __ who came to me and said, _____

44

"Hard work good _ and hard work fine, but first take care of head." _

Guitar Solo

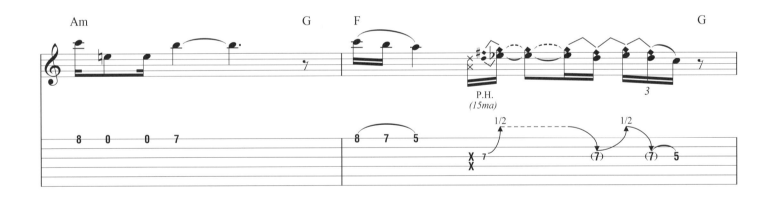

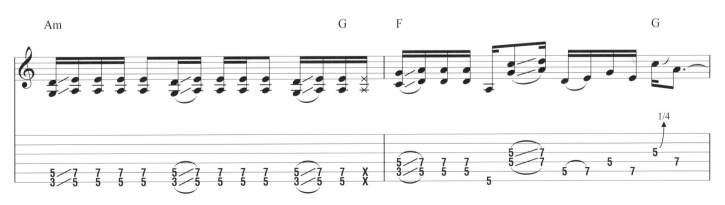

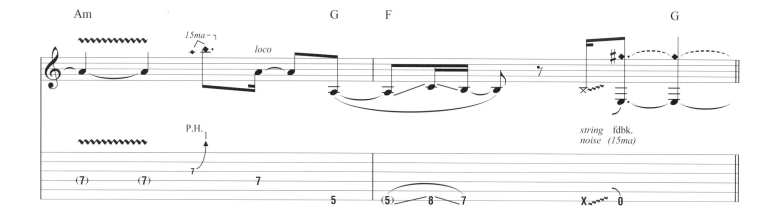

Interlude

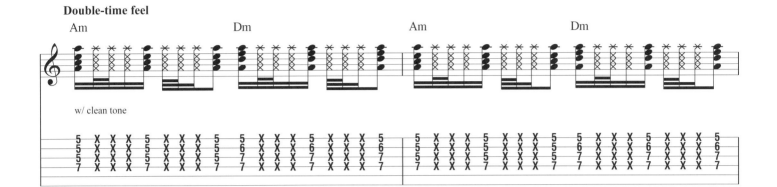

Double-time feel

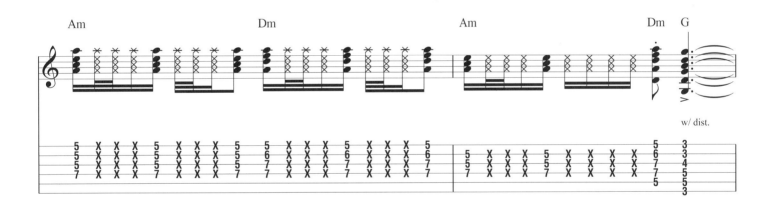

Freely

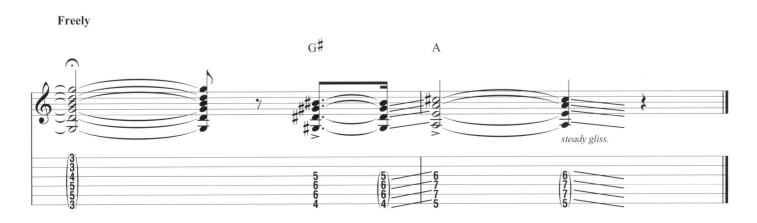

STP

Words and Music by Brad Nowell

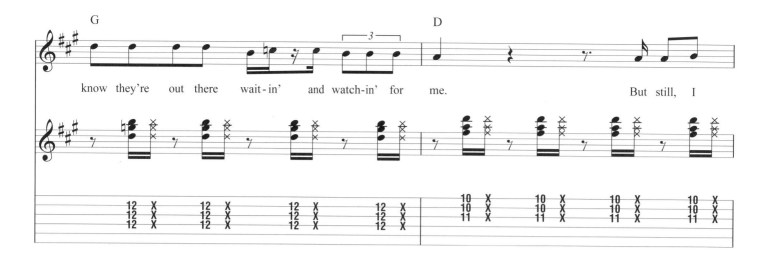

know they're out there wait-in' and watch-in' for me.   But still, I

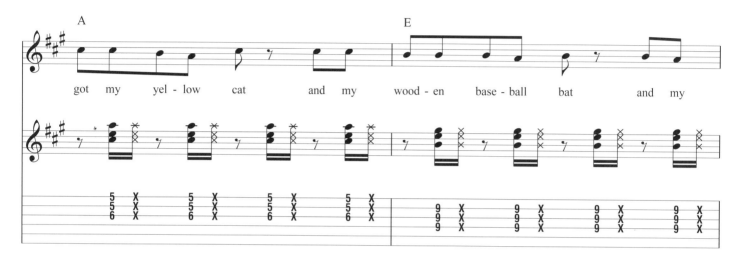

got my yel - low cat   and my wood - en base - ball bat   and my

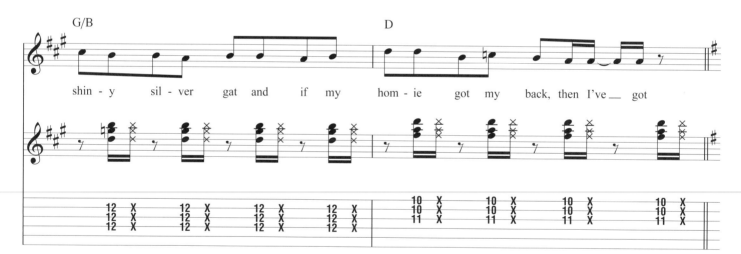

shin - y sil - ver gat and if my hom - ie got my back, then I've __ got

Chorus

all, _____   uh, that I   need. _____   Uh,

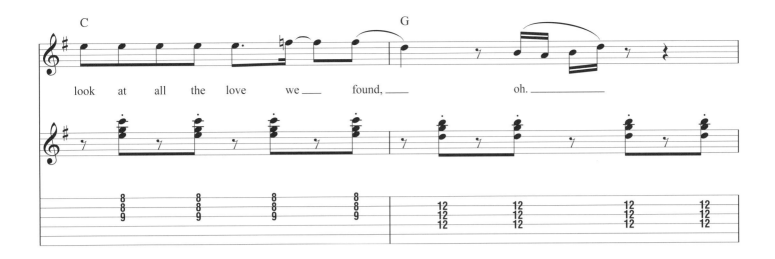

look at all the love we ___ found, ___ oh. ___

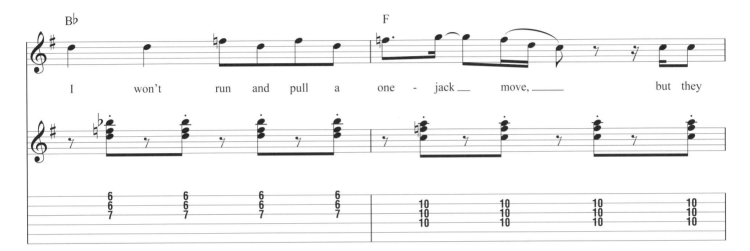

I won't run and pull a one - jack ___ move, ___ but they

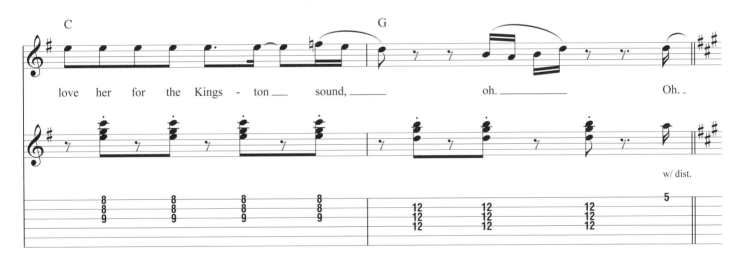

love her for the Kings - ton ___ sound, ___ oh. ___ Oh. ___

w/ dist.

Interlude

Oh. ___

let ring -

And if she made out with my last clean rig, I'm gon-na kill that

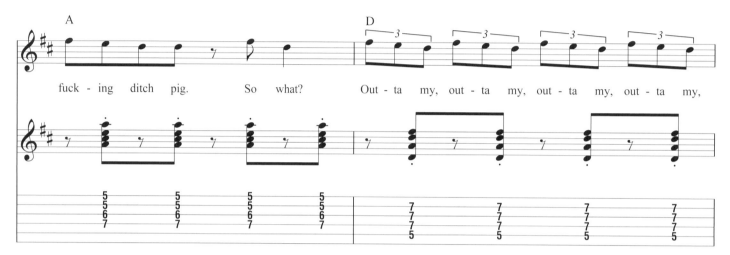

fuck-ing ditch pig. So what? Out-ta my, out-ta my, out-ta my, out-ta my,

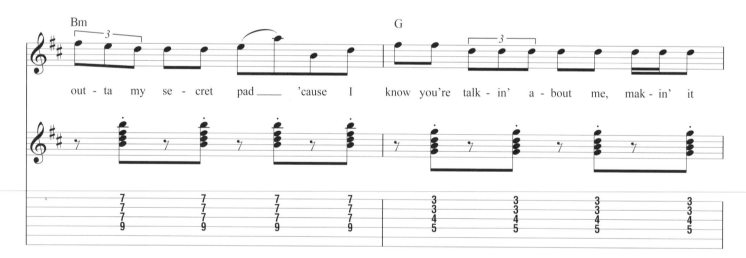

out-ta my se-cret pad ___ 'cause I know you're talk-in' a-bout me, mak-in' it

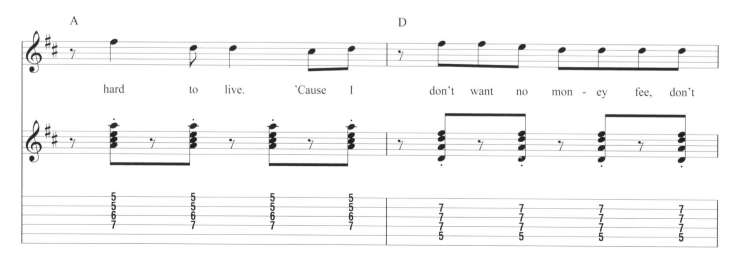

hard to live. 'Cause I don't want no mon-ey fee, don't

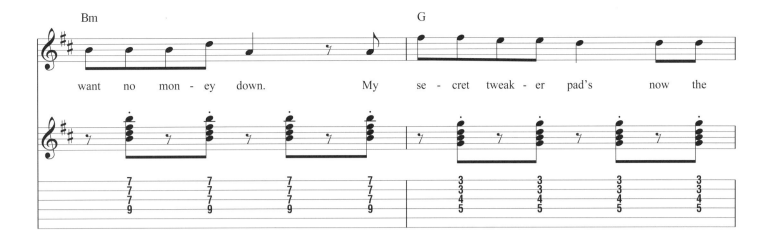

want no mon-ey down. My se-cret tweak-er pad's now the

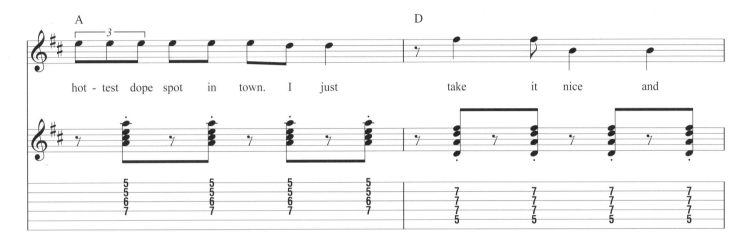

hot-test dope spot in town. I just take it nice and

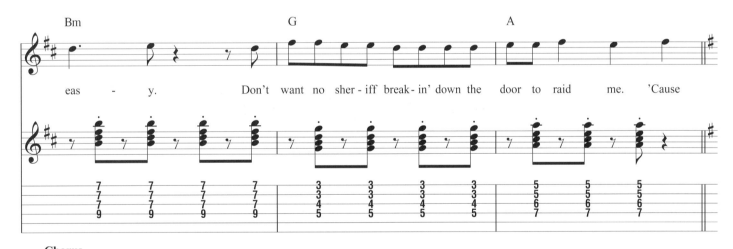

eas - y. Don't want no sher-iff break-in' down the door to raid me. 'Cause

Chorus
Tempo I

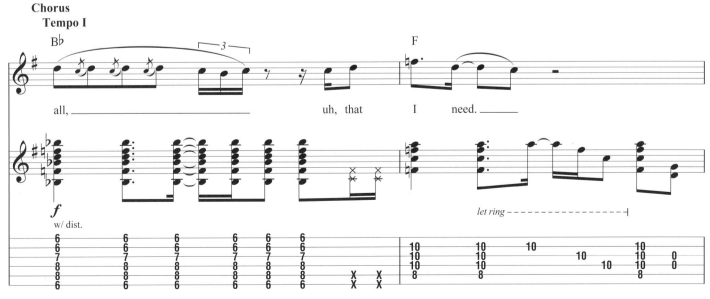

all, uh, that I need.

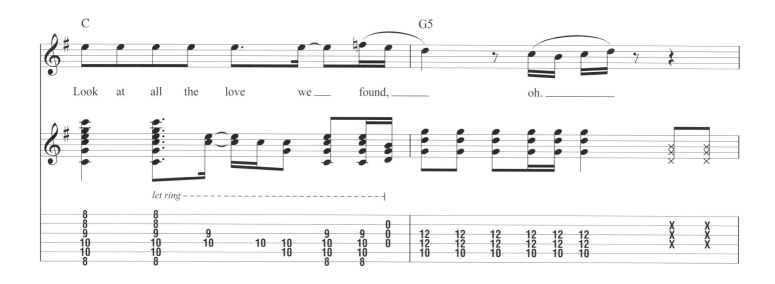

Look at all the love we ___ found, ___ oh. ___

Double-time feel

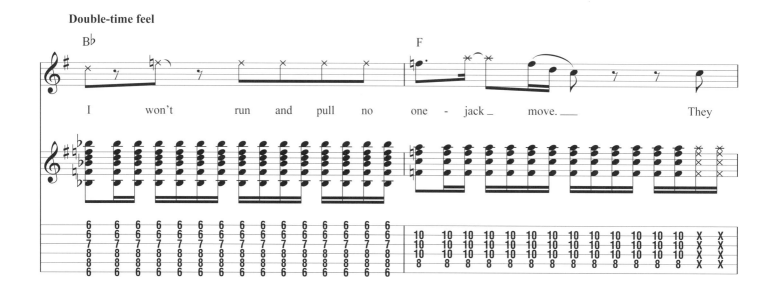

I won't run and pull no one - jack ___ move. ___ They

End double-time feel

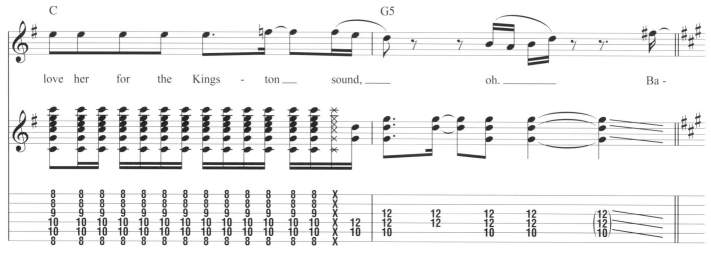

love her for the Kings - ton ___ sound, ___ oh. ___ Ba -

What I Got

Words and Music by Brad Nowell, Eric Wilson, Floyd Gaugh and Lindon Roberts

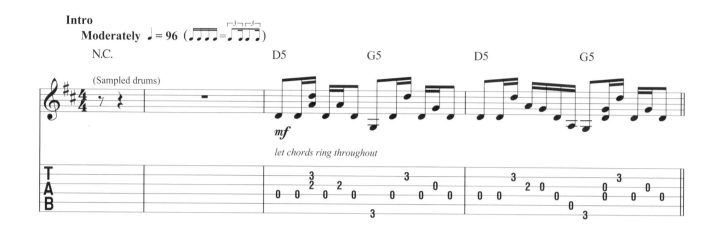

1. Early in the morn-in', ris-in' to __ the street. __

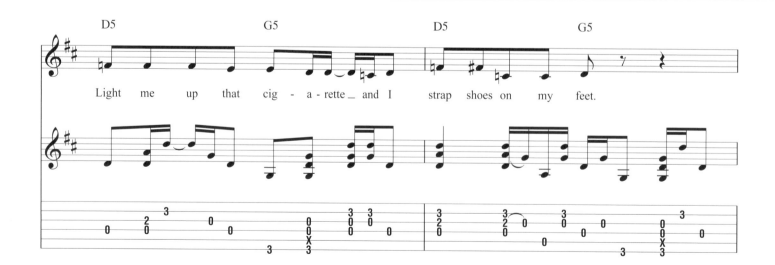

Light me up that cig-a-rette __ and I strap shoes on my feet.

Got to find a rea - son, rea - son things _ went wrong. _

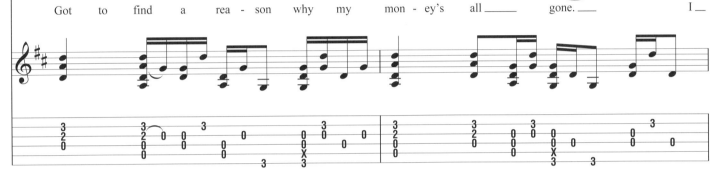

Got to find a rea - son why my mon - ey's all _____ gone. _____ I _

_____ got a Dal - ma - tion, and I can still _ get high. _ I _

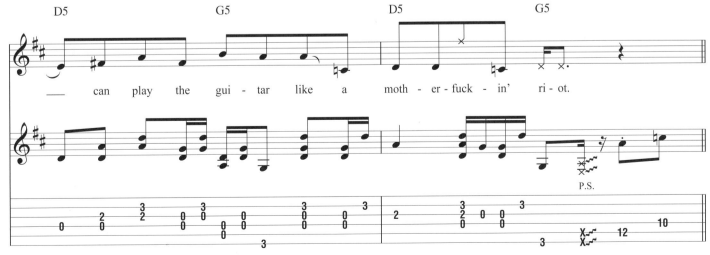

_____ can play the gui - tar like a moth - er - fuck - in' ri - ot.

Guitar Solo

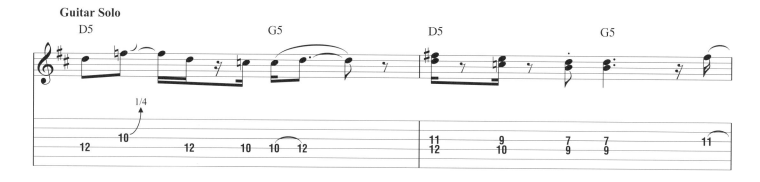

2. Well, life

is   so love _ the one you got 'cause you might get run o - ver or you might   get   shot.
(too short)

Verse

Nev-er start no stat-ic, I just get it off my __
(chest.)

Nev-er had to bat-tle with no bul-let-proof
(vest.)

*Tap body of guitar.

Chorus

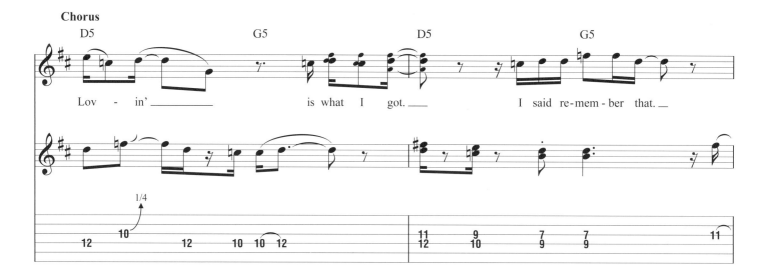

Lov - in' _____ is what I got. ___ I said re-mem-ber that. ___

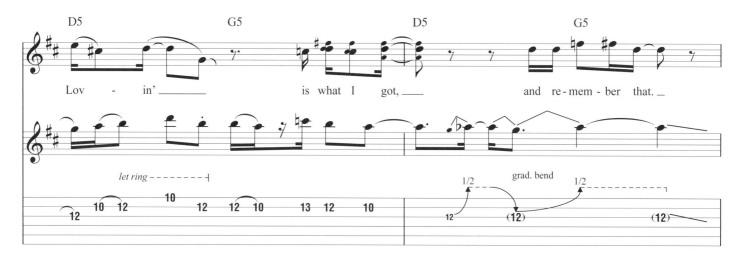

Lov - in' _____ is what I got, ___ and re-mem-ber that. ___

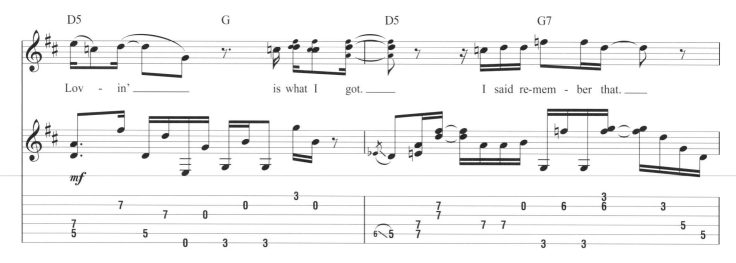

Lov - in' _____ is what I got. ___ I said re-mem - ber that. ___

Lov - in' _____ is what I got, ___ I got, ___ I got, ___ I got.

Verse

3. Why I don't cry when my dog runs _ a-way. I don't get an-gry at the bills I have _ to pay.

I don't get an-gry when my mom smokes pot, hits the bot-tle and goes right to the rock.

Fuck-in' and fight-in', it's all the same. Liv-in' with Lou-ie Dog's the on-ly way to stay sane.

Let the lov-in', let _ the lov-in' _ come back _ to me. _

Interlude

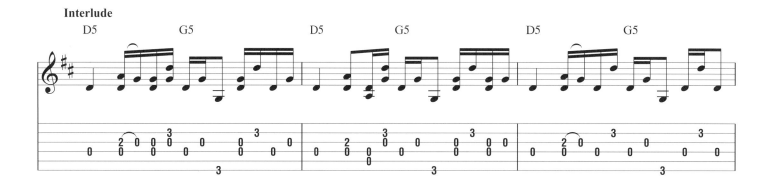

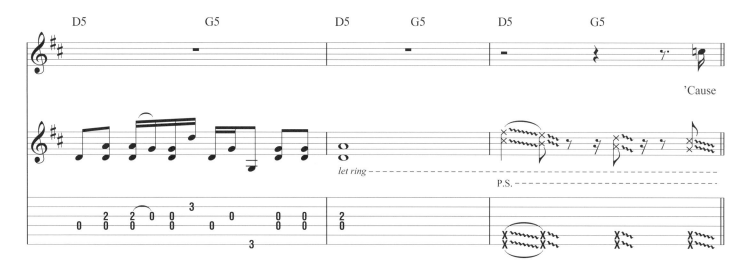

'Cause

Chorus

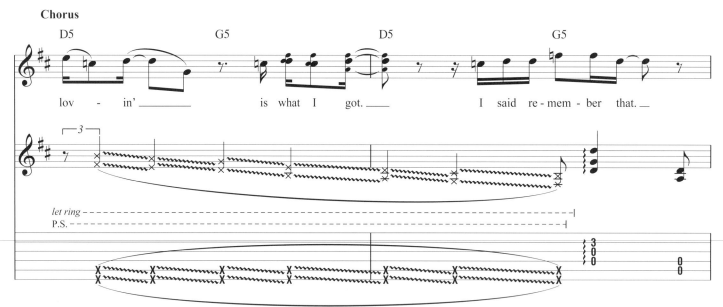

lov - in' _____ is what I got. ___ I said re - mem - ber that. __

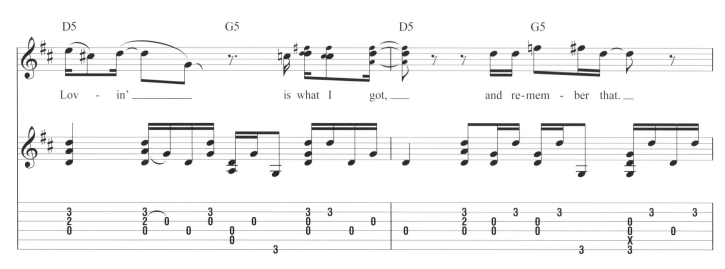

Lov - in' _____ is what I got, ___ and re - mem - ber that. __

Lov - in' _____ is what I got, ___ now. I said re-mem - ber that. ___

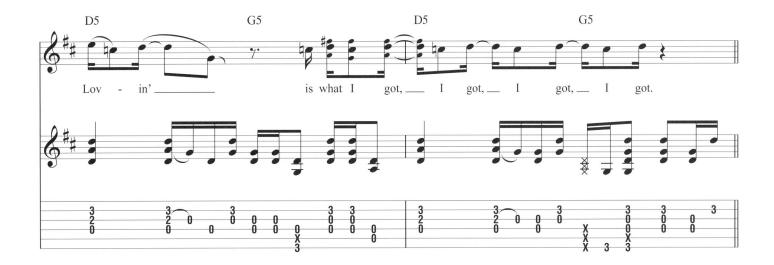

Lov - in' _____ is what I got, ___ I got, ___ I got, ___ I got.

Outro

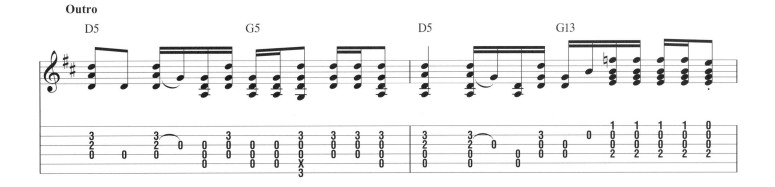

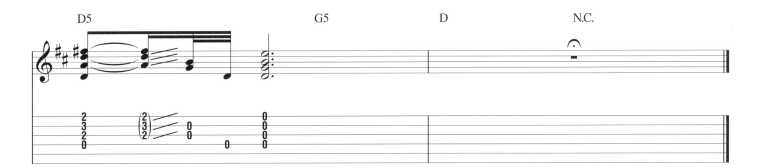

Wrong Way

Words and Music by Brad Nowell, Eric Wilson and Floyd Gaugh

Verse
Faster ♩ = 148

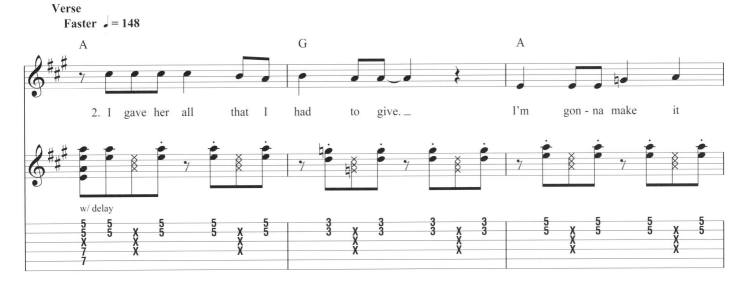

2. I gave her all that I had to give. _ I'm gon - na make it

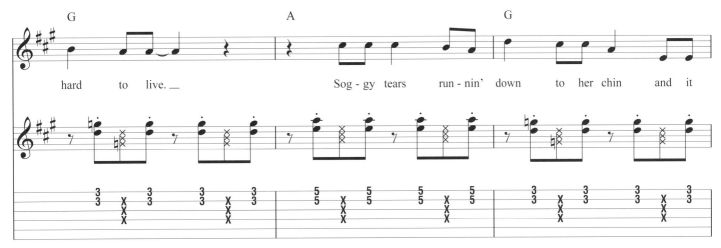

hard to live. _ Sog - gy tears run - nin' down to her chin and it

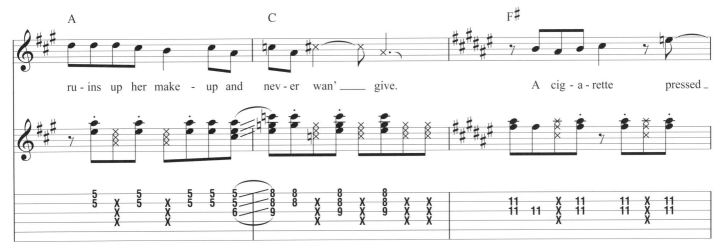

ru - ins up her make - up and nev - er wan' _ give. A cig - a - rette pressed _

_ be - tween her lips but I'm star - in' at her tits. It's the wrong way. _

67

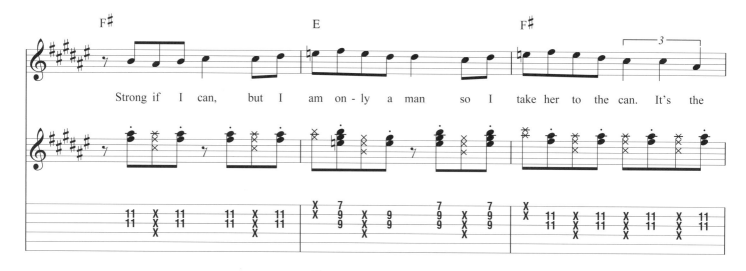

Strong if I can, but I am on-ly a man so I take her to the can. It's the

Verse

wrong way. ___ 3. The on-ly fam-i-ly that she's ev-er had is her

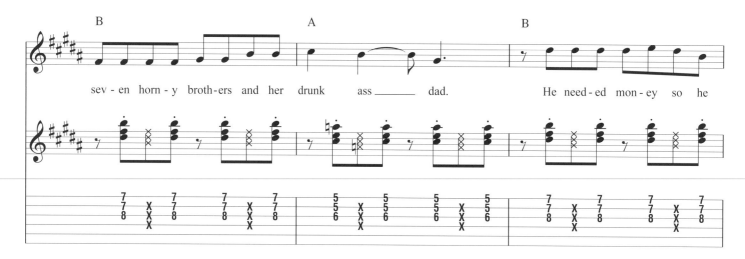

sev-en horn-y broth-ers and her drunk ass ___ dad. He need-ed mon-ey so he

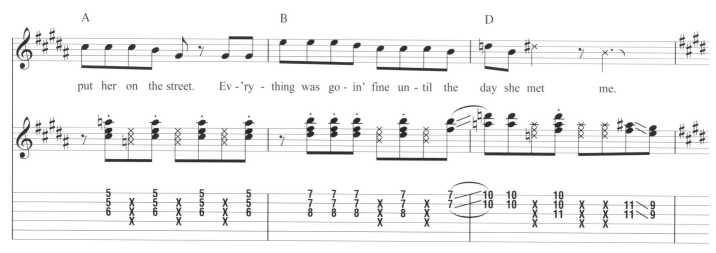

put her on the street. Ev-'ry-thing was go-in' fine un-til the day she met me.

Hap - py, are you sad? Wan - na shoot your dad? I'll do an - y - thing I can the

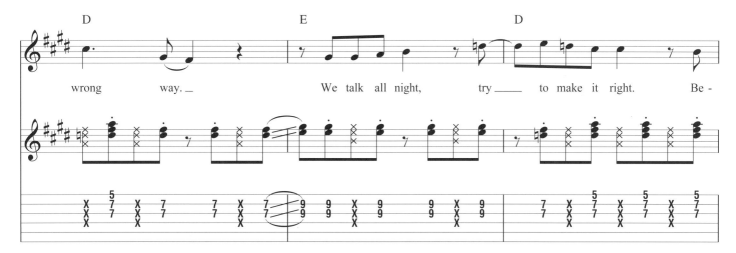

wrong way. __ We talk all night, try __ to make it right. Be -

Verse

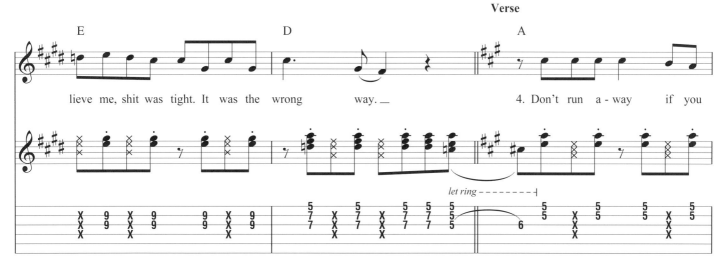

lieve me, shit was tight. It was the wrong way. __ 4. Don't run a - way if you

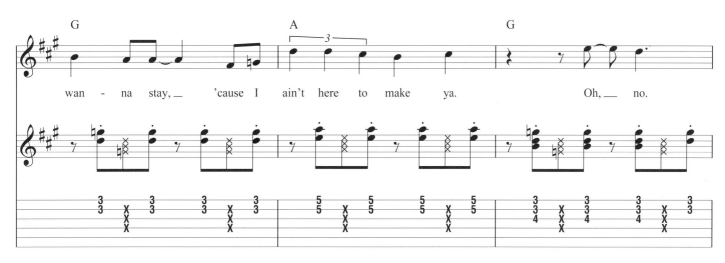

wan - na stay, __ 'cause I ain't here to make ya. Oh, __ no.

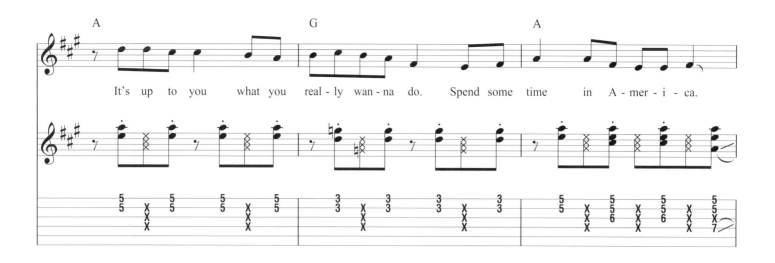

It's up to you what you real-ly wan-na do. Spend some time in A-mer-i-ca.

Trombone Solo

Ha, dub __ style!

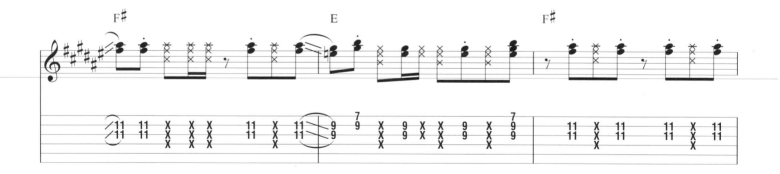

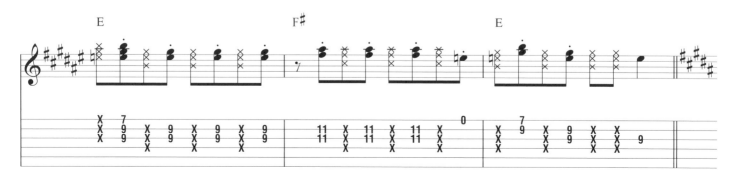

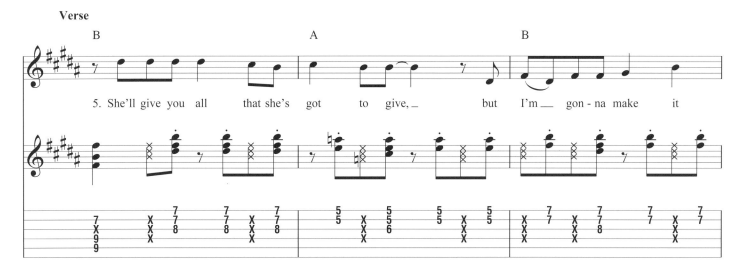

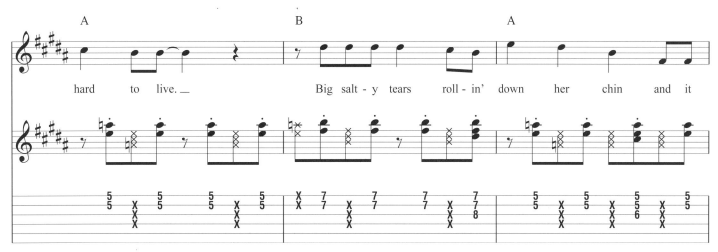

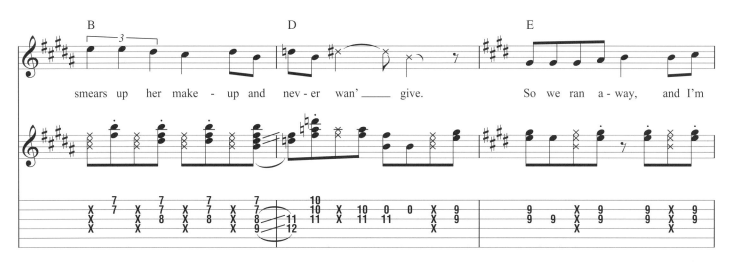

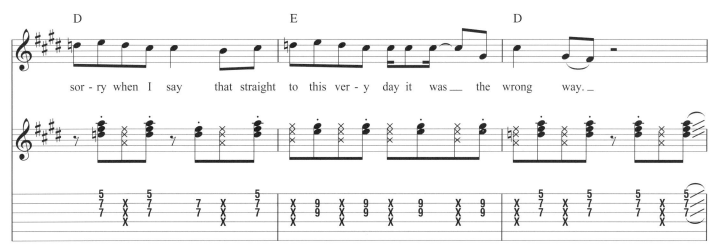

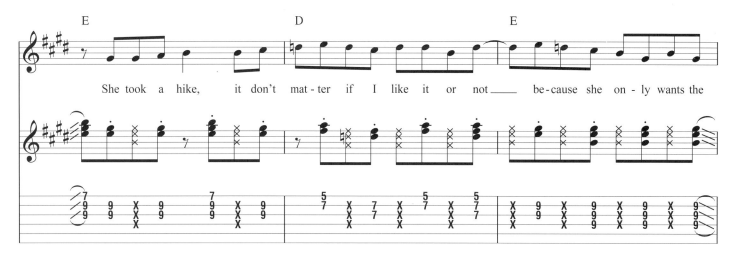

She took a hike, it don't mat-ter if I like it or not___ be-cause she on-ly wants the

Verse

wrong way.___   6. I gave her all that I had to give,___ but she

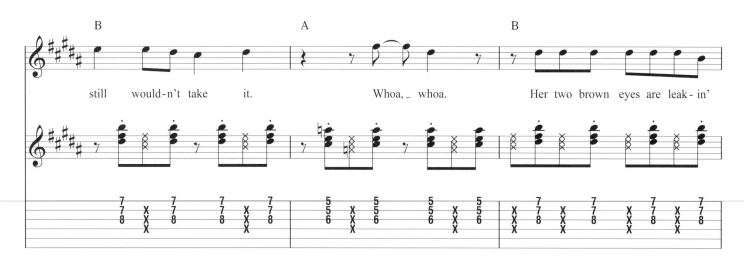

still would-n't take it.   Whoa,___ whoa.   Her two brown eyes are leak-in'

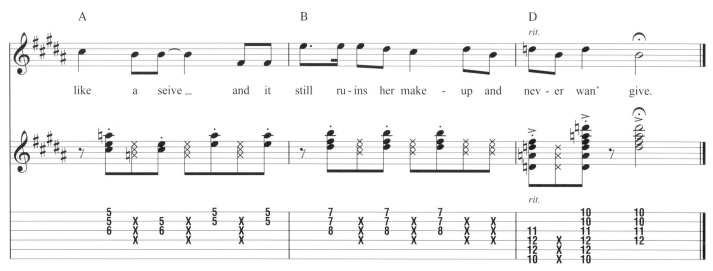

like a seive___ and it still ru-ins her make-up and nev-er wan' give.